Edward Lear's ALPHABET of Nonsense

with an Introduction by
Colin Harrison

ASHMOLEAN MUSEUM

Edward Lear's Alphabet of Nonsense:
A facsimile from the 1862 edition in the Ashmolean Museum

The Ashmolean Museum, Oxford

Copyright Ashmolean Museum, University of Oxford, 2012

British Library Cataloguing in Publications Data

A catalogue record for this book is available from the British Library

EAN 13: 978 1 85444 271 0

Catalogue designed in Momotype Modern
by Geoff Green Book Design, Cambridge

Printed and bound in Malta by Gutenberg Press

For further details of Ashmolean titles please visit:
www.ashmolean.org/shop

Throughout his life, Edward Lear (1812–1888) sought recognition as a serious professional artist. He was essentially self-taught, but by the age of nineteen, he was working on his Illustrations of the Family of Psittacidae, or Parrots. This volume was published in parts between 1830 and 1832. The extraordinary quality and accuracy of Lear's plates brought him to the attention of a number of influential figures, among them the 13th Earl of Derby, whose menagerie at Knowsley Hall near Liverpool was the most important in Europe. Lear made drawings and watercolours of a wide range of animals, some of which were eventually published as *Gleanings from the*

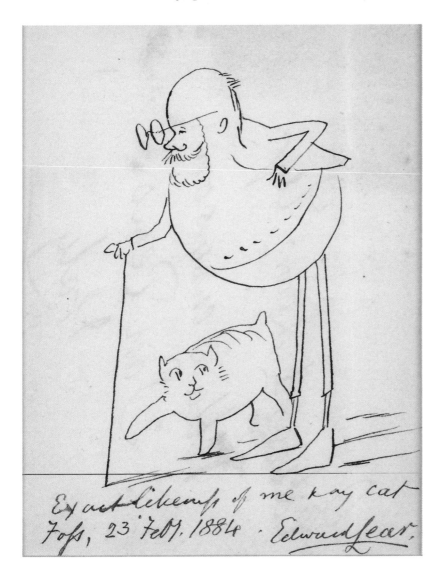

Menagerie at Knowsley in 1846. In 1837, Lear abandoned ornithology and natural history, claiming that his eyesight was no longer adequate, and travelled to Italy for the sake of his health. He settled in Rome, and made his reputation as a landscape artist, first in drawings and lithographs, and later in watercolours and oils. Over the next forty years, he travelled more extensively than almost any other artist, making expeditions to Greece and Albania, Turkey and Egypt and the Near East, and even venturing as far as India in 1873–5. For some years, he made his home in Corfu, but he later lived at San Remo on the Italian Riviera together with his beloved cat, Foss.

It was while he was staying at Knowsley that Lear began to amuse himself and Lord Derby's children by making nonsense rhymes illustrated by his own drawings. His

humour when in company was irrepressible, and both adults and children delighted in his facility for creating new words, finding absurdity in everyday objects, and placing people in improbable situations. The rhymes are now known as Limericks, but this was not a term that was ever used in Lear's lifetime. Although most of the nonsense was invented for specific children on particular occasions, Lear published some of his best rhymes in *A Book of Nonsense* in 1846, using the pseudonym Derry Down Derry, taken from a character in the mediaeval mummers' plays. This edition was published using lithography, and it is generally assumed that no more than a few hundred copies were printed. A new edition was published in 1855, under the same pseudonym and again in a limited number of copies, and it was not until the third and much expanded edition, of 1861, that Lear's name appeared on the title page. For the first time, Lear's drawings were reproduced by wood engraving, a technique which allowed the publication of enormous numbers of copies. From that date, Lear's reputation as a nonsense writer began to eclipse his standing as a landscape painter. He later published nonsense in other genres, notably *Nonsense Songs*,

Stories, Botany, and Alphabets in 1871, which included for the first time 'The Owl and the Pussy-Cat'.

Most of Lear's nonsense alphabets date from the mid-1850s, when he first acknowledged that he was the author of *A Book of Nonsense* by giving presentation copies to many of his wide circle of friends. Six alphabets were published in the posthumous edition of *Nonsense Botany and Nonsense Alphabets* (1889), and several others survive. The texts and drawings illustrating each letter vary considerably: one has a verse of four lines, one a verse of seven with rhymes consisting of a single word repeated with a different initial letter, and one has no verse or drawing at all, but is a continuous story using each letter to introduce a different sentence. The best of the alphabets, however, repeat the letter in the penultimate line.

The present nonsense alphabet was made for Ruth Decie. Her parents, Captain Richard Decie and his wife Bella, were stationed in the British garrison on Corfu and they and their young son Frank became close friends of Lear's in the winter of 1861–2. Lear already knew Mrs Decie's parents, William and Arabella Prescott, who lived in Roehampton, Surrey. Clarence House, or 'Hospitality Hall', as Lear christened it, offered exactly the kind of domestic comfort that Lear enjoyed best, and he stayed there several times. W.G. Prescott was a partner in the private bank of Prescott, Grote, Cave, and Co., and 'a hearty, gentlemanly man', the head of a 'merry & pleasant family' who were 'very jovial, hospitable folk'. Indeed, Lear went so far as

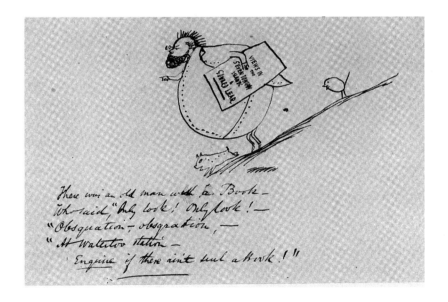

to write that 'I have never really known such people as
these, embodying wealth & simplicity, & immense kindli-
ness'. The Prescotts became collectors of Lear's landscapes
and subscribed to *Views in the Seven Ionian Islands*, and
their wide circle included many artists and writers who
were also friends of Lear's. His first visit took place from
Saturday to Monday, 21 to 23 June 1862 and, in spite of
the extremely cold and grey weather, passed very pleas-
antly. Lear recorded in his diary for 22 June 1862 that he
'rose at 6:30 & made an alphabet for the Decie baby till 9',
and completed it after lunch. Unusually, a draught of the
alphabet survives, in the Houghton Library, Harvard, and
shows that he must have first made the verses for each letter, then copied them out with rough drawings, and made
the fair copy with careful drawings on blue, linen-backed
writing paper after lunch. The subjects are a typical mix-
ture of animals and domestic articles that would be familiar
to any child, and only at the letters u, x, and z was Lear
obliged to look beyond these narrow horizons. The choice
of a ukase to illustrate the letter u is particularly unex-
pected, but it may have been prompted by such an edict
found in a bookcase at Clarence House itself. Certainly,
when Lear came to redraw this alphabet for publication in
1871, he replaced the ukase with a 'useful old urn', which
would have been rather more familiar to his readers. The
published version loses something of the spontaneity of
Lear's drawings, and especially the animation on the faces
of the animals, the slightly dotty duck and quail, the vac-
uous fish, the curious and alert jackdaw, the stolid elephant
and tortoise. Above all, the rabbit, supremely self-satisfied
as it feasts on garden flowers, is one of Lear's most endear-
ing creations.

Lear's alphabet, together with illustrated letters, a suite
of four 'Eggstracts from the Roehampton Chronicle', and
other items, became treasured family heirlooms, passing
from the Decies to James Farquharson, who bequeathed
many of them, including the alphabet, to the Ashmolean
Museum in 2011.

Edward Lear's
ALPHABET
of Nonsense

A was some Ants,
Who seldom stood still
And they made a nice house
On the side of the hill.

a.

busy old Ants!

A was some Ants,
Who seldom stood still
And they made a nice house
On the side of a hill.

A.

busy old Ants!

B

B was a Book,
With a binding of blue
And pictures: and stories
For me and for you

b!

Nice little book

B

B was a Book,
With a binding of blue
And pictures: and stories
For me and for you.

b!

Nice little book!

C

C was a Cat,
Who ran after a Rat
But his courage did fail
When he seized on his tail

C!
Crafty old Cat!

C

C was a Cat,
Who ran after a Rat
But his courage did fail,
When she seized on his tail.

C!
Crafty old Cat!

D

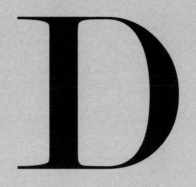

D was a Duck,
With spots on his back.
He lived in the water,
and always said Quack

D

dear little duck!

D

D was a Duck,
With spots on his back.
He lived in the water,
And always said Quack!
D,
dear little duck!

E was an Elephant,
Stately and wise,
He wore tusks and a trunk,
And 2 queer litle eyes

e

O! what funny small eyes!

E. was an Elephant,
Stately and wise,
He wore tusks and a trunk,
And 2 queer little Eyes.

E. !

O! what funny small eyes!

F was a Fish,
Who was caught in a net
But he got out again,
And is quite alive yet

f!
lively old fish!

F

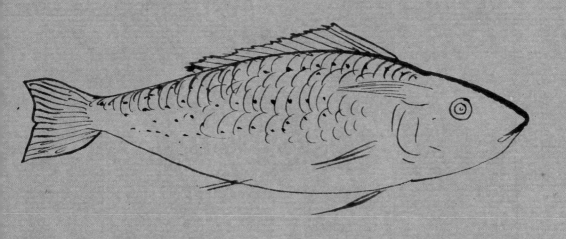

F was a Fish,
Who was caught in a net
But he got out again,
And is quite alive yet.

f!

lively old fish!

G

G was a Goat
Who was spotted with brown.
When he did not lie still,
He walked up and down.

G!

good little goat!

G

G was a Goat
Who was spotted with brown:
When he did not lie still,
He walked up and down.

G!
good little goat!

H

H was a Hat
Which was all on one side,
Its' crown was too high,
And its' brim was too wide

h!
Handsome old hat!

H

H was a Hat
Which was all on one side,
Its crown was too high,
And its brim was too wide.

h!

Handsome old hat!

I

I was some Ice
So white and so nice
But which nobody tasted,
And so it was wasted,

i

All that good ice!

I

I was some Ice
So white and so nice
But which nobody tasted,
And so it was wasted,
i —
All that good ice!

J

J was a Jackdaw
Who hopped up and down,
In the principal street
Of a neighbouring town.

j!
Jacky-jo-jown!

J

J. was a Jackdaw
Who hopped up and down,
In the principal street
Of a neighbouring town.
J. !
Jacky-jo-jown!

K

K was a Kite
Which flew out of sight
Above houses so high
All into the sky

k!

Fly away kite!

K

K was a kite
Which flew out of sight
Above houses so high
All into the sky.

k !
Fly away kite !

L

L was a Light
Which burned all the night,
And illumined the gloom
Of a very dark room.

l!

Valuable light!

L

L was a Light
Which burned all the night,
And illumined the gloom
Of a very dark room.

l !

Valuable light !

M

M was a Mill,
Which turned round and round
As fast as could be
With a loud hummy sound.

m

Merry old mill!

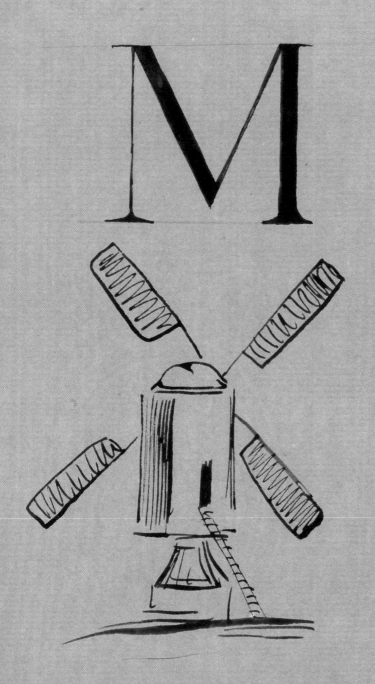

M

M. was a Mill,
Which turned round and round
As fast as could be
With a loud hummy sound.
M.
Merry old mill!

N

 was a net
Which caught some small fish
And because they were wet
They were put in a dish.

n

nice little net!

nice little net

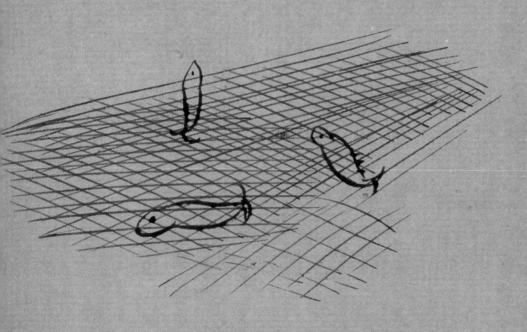

N. was a net
Which caught some small fish
And because they were wet
They were put in a dish.

N.

nice little net!

O was an Orange
So yellow and round,
When it fell off the tree,
It fell down to the ground

O!

Down to the ground!

O

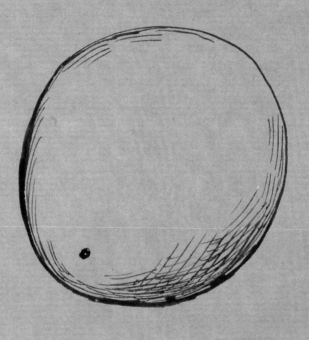

O was an Orange
So yellow and round;
When it fell off the tree,
It fell down to the ground.
O!
Down to the ground!

P

P was a Pig
Who was not very big,
But his tail was too curly
And that made him surly

p!

poor little pig!

P

P was a Pig
who was not very big,
But his tail was too curly
And that made him surly.

p!
poor little pig!

Q was a Quail
With a very short tail
For he fed upon Corn,
Ever since he was born.

q!

Quaint little quail!

Qwas a Quail
With a very short tail
For he fed upon Corn,
Ever since he was born.

Q !

Quaint little quail !

R

R was a Rabbit
Who had a bad habit
Of eating the flowers,
In gardens and bowers.

r

Naughty fat rabbit!

R

R. was a Rabbit
Who had a bad habit
Of eating the flowers,
In gardens and bowers.

r!

naughty fat rabbit!

S was a Sugar tongs,
Nippity-nee,
To take up the sugar,
And put in your tea.

S

Sugar-go-gee!

S

S was a Sugar-tongs,
Nippity-nee,
To take up the sugar,
And put in your tea.
S.
Sugar-go-gee!

T

T was a Tortoise,
All yellow and black
But he walked quite away,
And he never came back.

t

torty never came back!

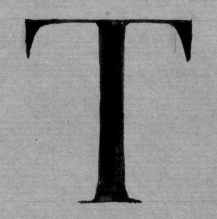

T was a Tortoise,
All yellow and black
But he walked quite away,
And he never came back.

T
torty never came back!

U

U was a Ukase
kept locked in a Book-case,
And sent by the Czar
to a province afar.

U!
Ugly old Ukase!

(In Imperial Russia, a Ukase was an edict or order
of the czar having the force of law)

U

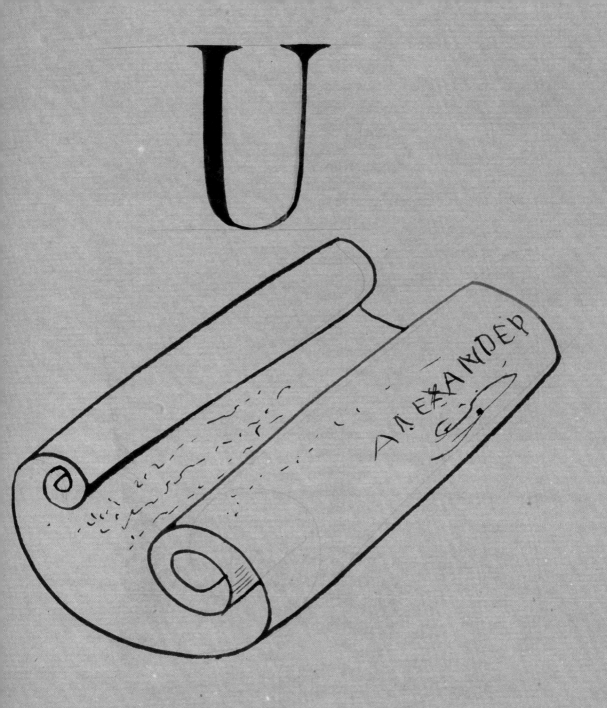

U was an Ukase
Kept locked in a Book-case,
And sent by the Czar
To a province afar.

U!

Ugly old Ukase!

V was a Villa,
Which stood on a hill,
By the side of a river
And close to a mill.

V!
Villa and mill

V

Villa and mill.

V. was a villa,
Which stood on a hill,
By the side of a river
And close to a mill.
V!
Villa and mill.

W

W was a Whale
With a very long tail
His ways were terrific
Throughout the Pacific!

W

Remarkable Whale!

W. was a Whale
With a very long tail
His ways were terrific
Throughout the Pacific!

W.

Remarkable whale!

X was King Xerces,
Who more than all Turks is
Renowned for his passion
And furious fashion.

x

angry old Xerces!

and furious

X

X . was King Xerxes,
Who more than all Turks is
Renowned for his passion
and furious fashion.

X
angry old Xerxes!

Y

Y was a Yew,
Which flourished and grew,
Near a quiet abode,
by the side of a road.

y!
pretty old Yew!

Y

Y. was a Yew,
Which flourished and grew,
near a quiet abode,
By the side of a road.

y!

Pretty old yew!

Z

Z was some Zinc,
So shining and bright,
Which caused you to wink
In the sun's pretty light.

Z
Beautiful zinc!

Z

Z. was some Zinc,
So shining and bright,
Which caused you to wink
In the sun's pretty light.

Z.

Beautiful Zinc!

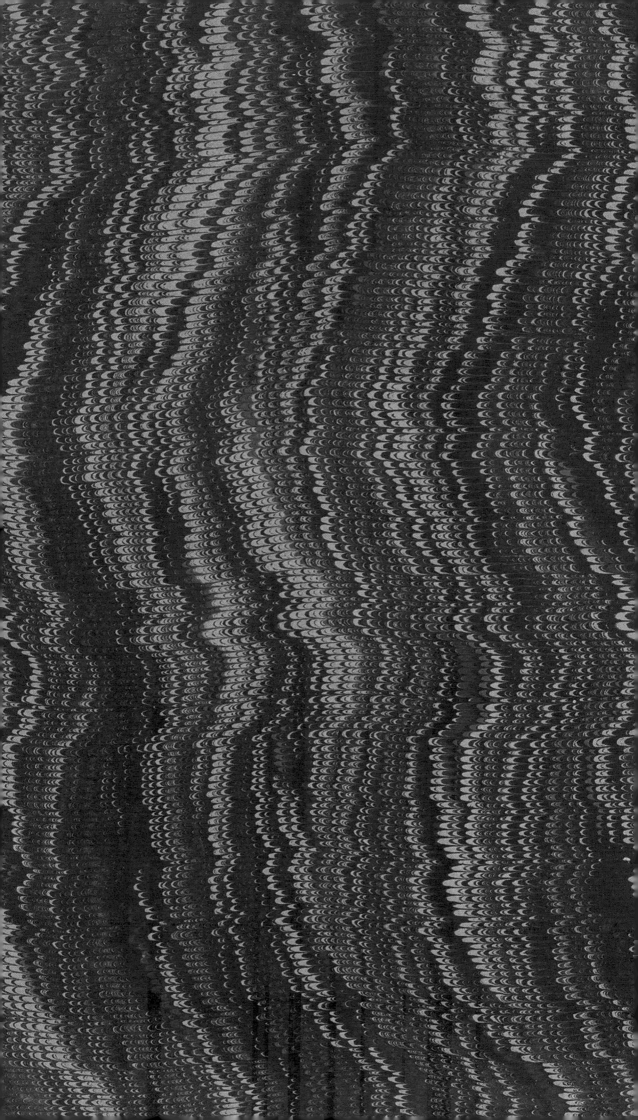